Handy South Dakota Genealogy Handbook

I0450616

Gary L. Morris

©2015 Gary L. Morris

ISBN-13: 978-1507759134

ISBN-10: 1507759134

Table of Contents

Notes

Genealogical Research in South Dakota

There are many historical and genealogical records and resources available for tracing your family history in South Dakota. Because of the abundance of information held at many different locations, tracking down the records for your ancestor can be an ominous task. Don't worry though, we know just where they are, and we'll show you which records you'll need, while helping you to understand:

1. What they are
2. Where to find them
3. How to use them

These records can be found both online and off, so we'll introduce you to online websites, indexes and databases, as well as brick-and-mortar repositories and other institutions that will help with your research in South Dakota. So that you will have a more comprehensive understanding of these records, we have provided a brief history of the "Mount Rushmore State" to illustrate what type of records may have been generated during specific time periods. That information will assist you in pinpointing times and locations on which to focus the search for your South Dakota ancestors and their records.

A Brief History of South Dakota

The area now known as South Dakota has been inhabited for over 25,000 years. The first people were nomadic groups of the Native Americans who European settlers would find there when they first arrived following the Lewis and Clark expedition of 1804-1806. The white settlers sought to dominate the Native tribes by negotiating peace treaties and converting them to the Christian faith. Most of the first whites to settle in the region were fur traders, who had by the mid 1850's had completely depleted all major sources of furs and hides. After the depletion of fur-providing animals, the white settlers turned their attention to usurping Indian lands and preparing ceded territories for more white settlers.

The Dakota Territory was established in 1861, and included much of present-day Montana and Wyoming as well as North and South Dakota. Seven years later Wyoming and Montana were eliminated from the Dakota Territory, and a gold rush six years after that brought thousands of prospectors and settlers to the area. South Dakota became a separate state in 1889 with Pierre as the capitol. There were nine Indian reservations included within the state, established after three wars with the Sioux and extensive negotiations.

Four reservations were established east of the Missouri for the Yankton and several Isanti Sioux tribes, and five reservations to the west of the Missouri for the Teton and Yanktonai Sioux. Sovereignty was thus divided among state officials, Indian agents, and tribal leaders, a division that did not always encourage efficient government. Through the late 19th and early 20th centuries, South Dakotans had limited economic opportunities, as agriculture was the primary industry. Close to 30,000 Sioux barely survived on livestock production and farming, inadequately supplemented by off-reservation employment and irregular government jobs. The 500,000 non-Indians lived mainly off mineral production (especially gold), small grain sales east of the Missouri, cattle-feeding enterprises, and a variety of service industries at urban centers throughout the state.

A tourism industry was established after World War I accompanied by efforts to subdue and harness the waters of the Missouri. Federal aid sustained the state through he Great Depression of the 1930's, thought he period after World War II saw an economic revival fueled by dam construction along the Missouri, rural electrification, arid-land reclamation, and the mechanization of agriculture. Federal programs saw many Native Americans relocated to urban centers where jobs and improved education were available, increasing occupational opportunities on reservations.

Important Dates in South Dakota History

1803 – Part of the Louisiana Purchase

1805 – Part of Louisiana Territory

1812 – Part of Missouri Territory

1821 – Part of unorganized Indian Territory

1934 – Part of Michigan Territory

1836 – Part of Wisconsin Territory

1838 – Part of Iowa Territory

1849 – Part of Minnesota Territory

1858 – White settlements established at Yankton and Vermillion

1861 – Reorganized as the Dakota Territory; included Montana and Wyoming

1864 – Montana and Wyoming separate from Dakota Territory

1875 – Gold discovered in Black Hills

1876 – Sioux War

1889 – North and South Dakota become separate states

1890 – Massacre of Lakota Indians at Wounded Knee

Famous Battles Fought in South Dakota

The **Battle of Slim Buttes** was fought in South Dakota during the Sioux War of 1876, while the **Massacre at Wounded Knee** in 1890 is probably the most famous of any conflict between US Troops and Native Americans.

These battle accounts that exist can be very effective in uncovering the military records of your ancestor. They can tell you what regiments fought in which battles, and often include the names and ranks of many officers and enlisted men.

Battle of Slim Buttes:
http://www.nrcprograms.org/site/PageServer?pagename=airc_hist_b
attleofslimbuttes

Massacre at Wounded Knee:
http://www.eyewitnesstohistory.com/knee.htm

Common South Dakota Genealogical Issues and Resources to Overcome Them

Boundary Changes: Boundary changes are a common obstacle when researching South Dakota ancestors. You could be searching for an ancestor's record in one county when in fact it is stored in a different one due to historical county boundary changes.

The **Atlas of Historical County Boundaries** can help you to overcome that problem. It provides a chronological listing of every boundary change that has occurred in the history of South Dakota.

Atlas of Historical County Boundaries: http://publications.newberry.org/ahcbp/pages/South_Dakota.html

Name Changes: Surname changes, variations, and misspellings can complicate genealogical research. It is important to check all spelling variations. Soundex, a program that indexes names by sound, is a useful first step, but you can't rely on it completely as some name variations result in different Soundex codes. The surnames could be different, but the first name may be different too. You can also find records filed under initials, middle names, and nicknames as well, so you will need to **get creative with surname variations** and spellings in order to cover all the possibilities. For help with surname variations read our instructional article on **How to Use Soundex**.

get creative with surname variations: http://obituarieshelp.org/blog/?p=634

How to Use Soundex: http://obituarieshelp.org/blog/?p=505

South Dakota Genealogical Organizations and Archives

Genealogical resources include not only records, but the organizations that house them, or can direct you to them. These institutions include: *Archives, Libraries, Genealogical Societies, Family History Centers, Universities, Churches, and Museums.*

Following are links to their websites, their physical addresses, and a summary of the records you can find there.

Archives and Libraries

South Dakota State Archives – Naturalization Records, Newspaper Database, Cemetery Records, Newspaper Surname Index, Biographical Files, Military Records, Census records, Native American resources

900 Governors Drive
Pierre, SD 57501
Phone: (605) 773-3804
Fax: (605) 773-6041
E-mail: archref@state.sd.us

South Dakota State Archives: http://history.sd.gov/Archives/

National Archives at Denver - Federal population censuses for all States, 1790-1930, Indexes for the 1880, 1900, 1910, and 1920 censuses, Revolutionary War records, Pension and bounty land warrant applications, Ship's passenger lists, Indian censuses

17101 Huron Street
Broomfield, CO 80023
Telephone: 303-604-4740
Fax: 303-407-5707

National Archives at Denver:
http://www.archives.gov/denver/public/genealogy.html

National Archives—Central Plains Region (Kansas City) -
Federal population censuses for all States, 1790-1930; indexes for
the 1880, 1900, 1910, and 1920 censuses, selected military service
records and indexes; selected pension and bounty-land warrant
applications; censuses and land allotment files for Native Americans.

400 West Pershing Road
Kansas City, MO 64108
Phone: (816) 268-8000

National Archives—Central Plains Region (Kansas City):
http://www.archives.gov/kansas-city/

I.D. Weeks Library
University of South Dakota – Historical maps, Manuscripts, Native
American materials, periodicals, local histories

414 E. Clark Street
Vermillion, SD 57069
Phone: (605) 677-5371
Fax: (605) 677-5488
E-mail: weeksref@usd.edu

University of South Dakota: http://www.usd.edu/library/archives-
and-special-collections.cfm

Center for Western Studies – Family histories, Historical
newspapers, Church records, Immigrant lists, Diaries, and Personal
papers and correspondences. Much of the material relates to Swedish
and Norwegian immigrants.

P.O. Box 727
Augustana College
Sioux Falls, SD 57197
Phone: (605) 336-4921
Fax: (605) 336-5447

Center for Western Studies: http://www.augie.edu/center-for-
western-studies/

Genealogical and Historical Societies

Genealogical and historical societies have access to extensive catalogues of genealogical data. They are also able to offer expert guidance for genealogical researchers. Many members are professional genealogists who are most willing to share their expertise in finding ancestors.

South Dakota Genealogical Society – Variety of genealogical resources for searching South Dakota ancestors

SD Genealogical Society
PO Box 1101
Pierre, SD 57501-1101

South Dakota Genealogical Society:
http://www.rootsweb.ancestry.com/~sdgs/index.html

Tri-State Genealogical Society (South Dakota, Wyoming, Montana) – Church and Cemetery index, Family histories, Surname index, Historical Newspaper collection, Obituaries index, County census reports

c/o Public Library
905 5th Ave
Belle Fourche, SD 57717

Tri-State Genealogical Society:
http://freepages.genealogy.rootsweb.ancestry.com/~tristate/?cj=1&n etid=cj&o_xid=0001231185&o_lid=0001231185&o_sch=Affiliate+ External

Society of Black Hills Pioneers – Variety of resources on early South Dakota settlers

P.O. Box 252
Heulett, Wyoming82720
Tel: 307-290-0935
Email: maupinc@crook1.com

Society of Black Hills Pioneers: http://blackhillspioneers.com/

South Dakota Mailing Lists

Mailing lists are internet based facilities that use email to distribute a single message to all who subscribe to it. When information on a particular surname, new records, or any other important genealogy information related to the mailing list topic becomes available, the subscribers are alerted to it. Joining a mailing list is an excellent way to stay up to date on South Dakota genealogy research topics. Rootsweb have an extensive listing of **South Dakota Mailing Lists** on a variety of topics.

South Dakota Mailing Lists:
http://lists.rootsweb.ancestry.com/index/usa/SD/misc.html

South Dakota Message Boards

A message board is another internet based facility where people can post questions about a specific genealogy topic and have it answered by other genealogists. If you have questions about a surname, record type, or research topic, you can post your question and other researchers and genealogists will help you with the answer. Be sure to check back regularly, as the answers are not emailed to you. The South Dakota message boards at **Rootsweb** are completely free to use.

Rootsweb:
http://boards.rootsweb.com/localities.northam.usa.states/mb.ashx

South Dakota Newspapers and Periodicals

Many genealogy periodicals and historical newspapers contain reprinted copies of family genealogies, transcripts of family Bible records, information about local records and archives, census indexes, church records, queries, land records, obituaries, court records, cemetery records, and wills. The following sites have historical South Dakota newspapers and periodicals that you can search online or on-site.

South Dakota State Archives – Searchable online database of historical South Dakota newspapers

900 Governors Drive
Pierre, SD 57501
Phone: (605) 773-3804
Fax: (605) 773-6041
E-mail: archref@state.sd.us

South Dakota State Archives: http://history.sd.gov/Archives/

Tri-State Genealogical Society (South Dakota, Wyoming, Montana) – Govert Advance 1928 to 1939, Castle Rock Press and Moreau News 1916 – 1926 Northern Butte County, Newell Irrigator and Castle Rock Press -- 1928 – 1930, Newell Valley Irrigator 1907 – 1927 , Newell Valley Irrigator 1932-1984, Butte County Valley Irrigator 1985-2004, Newell Reclamation News 1915-1917

c/o Public Library
905 5th Ave
Belle Fourche, SD 57717

Tri-State Genealogical Society:
http://freepages.genealogy.rootsweb.ancestry.com/~tristate/?cj=1&netid=cj&o_xid=0001231185&o_lid=0001231185&o_sch=Affiliate+External

GenealogyBank.com – free searchable database of South Dakota newspaper archives, 1861–2002

GenealogyBank.com:
http://www.genealogybank.com/gbnk/newspapers/explore/USA/South_Dakota/

The Online Books Page – links to historical South Dakota books and periodicals available for viewing online

The Online Books Page:
http://onlinebooks.library.upenn.edu/webbin/book/browse?type=subject&c=c&key=south+dakota

Library of Congress Digital Newspaper Directory – free searchable database of historical U.S. newspapers dating from 1690-present

Library of Congress Digital Newspaper Directory:
http://chroniclingamerica.loc.gov/search/titles/

NewspaperArchive.com – largest online database of historical newspapers in the world.

NewspaperArchive.com: http://newspaperarchive.com/

Historical South Dakota Maps and Gazetteers

Maps are an integral part of genealogical research. They help us to
locate landmarks, towns, cities, parishes, states, provinces,
waterways and roads and streets. They also help us to determine
when and where boundary changes might have taken place, and give
us a visualization of the area we're researching in.

For locating place names, a gazetteer is the best possible resource for
any genealogist. Gazetteers are also sometimes called "place name
dictionaries", and can help you to locate the area in which you need
to conduct research. Below are links to the maps and gazetteers for
research in South Dakota.

Peabody GNIS Service – South Dakota:
http://peabody.research.yale.edu/cgi-
bin/Query.GNIS?ST=South%20Dakota&SU=1

Color Landform Atlas – South Dakota:
http://fermi.jhuapl.edu/states/sd_0.html

1985 U.S. Atlas link to: http://www.livgenmi.com/1895/SD/

South Dakota Hometown Locator:
http://southdakota.hometownlocator.com/

<u>South Dakota City Directories</u>

City directories are similar to telephone directories in that they list the residents of a particular area. The difference though is what is important to genealogists, and that is they pre-date telephone directories. You can find an ancestor's information such as their street address, place of employment, occupation, or the name of their spouse. A one-stop-shop for finding city directories in South Dakota is the **South Dakota Online Historical Directories** which contains a listing of every available online historical directory related to South Dakota. Another useful site is **US City Directories** which identifies printed, microfilmed, and online South Dakota directories and their repositories.

South Dakota Online Historical Directories:
https://sites.google.com/site/onlinedirectorysite/Home/usa/sd

US City Directories: http://www.uscitydirectories.com/sd.htm

South Dakota Genealogical Records

<u>Birth, Death, Marriage and Divorce Records</u> – Also known as vital records, birth, death, and marriage certificates are the most basic, yet most important records attached to your ancestor. The reason for their importance is that they not only place your ancestor in a specific place at a definite time, but potentially connect the individual to other relatives. Below is a list of repositories and websites where you can find South Dakota vital records.

South Dakota Department of Health – Birth, Death, Marriage, and Divorce records after 1905. Many birth records for events occurring before 1905 were filed later and are in the system. For births older than 100 years, visit their **Searchable Database**.

Office of Vital Records
600 East Capitol Avenue
Pierre, SD 57501-2536
Tel: 605-773-3361 or 1-800-738-2301 (In State)
Email: DOH.info@state.sd.us

South Dakota Department of Health: http://doh.sd.gov/records/

Searchable Database:
http://apps.sd.gov/applications/PH14Over100BirthRec/index.aspx

South Dakota State Historical Society - birth,death, and marriages from newspapers 1781-2009

900 Governors Drive,
Pierre, SD 57501, United States
Tel:605-773-3458

South Dakota State Historical Society: http://history.sd.gov/

Census Records

Census records are among the most important genealogical documents for placing your ancestor in a particular place at a specific time. Like BDM records, they can also lead you to other ancestors, particularly those who were living under the authority of the head of household.

National Archives at Denver - Federal population censuses for all States, 1790-1930

17101 Huron Street
Broomfield, CO 80023
Telephone: 303-604-4740
Fax: 303-407-5707

National Archives at Denver:
http://www.archives.gov/denver/public/genealogy.html

National Archives—Central Plains Region (Kansas City) - Federal population censuses for all States, 1790-1930; indexes for the 1880, 1900, 1910, and 1920 censuses, censuses and land allotment files for Native Americans.

400 West Pershing Road
Kansas City, MO 64108
Phone: (816) 268-8000

National Archives—Central Plains Region (Kansas City):
http://www.archives.gov/kansas-city/

The **Family History Library** in Salt Lake City, Utah has the following Indian Census Rolls on microfilm:

Supplemental census, births and deaths,1946-1948; Indian census rolls, Crow Creek, 1886-1942; Census of Yankton Reservation, 1931; Tribal census, 1886-1942; Indian census rolls, 1910,1911,1921,1924; Indian census rolls, Yankton, 1885-1931; Register of Lower Yantonai Sioux families, ca.1901; Indian census rolls, Santee, 1885-1917; Tribal census of the Lower Yantonai Sioux, 1895-1940; Tribal census, 1877; Indian census rolls, Flandreau, 1892-1939; Census records, 1876-1939; Lists of males over 18 years of age; 1889, Census records, 1874-1932; Indian census rolls, Cheyenne River, 1886-1942

Family History Library:
http://familysearch.org/learn/wiki/en/Family_History_Library

The **Free Census Project** has transcribed many South Dakota indexes and new material is added daily

Free Census Project: http://usgwcensus.org/cenfiles/sd.htm

Access Genealogy – South Dakota county census records dating from 1880

Access Genealogy: http://www.accessgenealogy.com/census/south-dakota-census-records.htm

African American Census Schedules Online – slave schedules, mortality schedules, slave-owners census

African American Census Schedules Online:
http://www.afrigeneas.com/aacensus/ga/

Native Americans in Census Records (US National Archives):
http://www.archives.gov/research/census/native-americans/

South Dakota Church Records

Church and synagogue records are a valuable resource, especially for baptisms, marriages, and burials that took place before 1900. You will need to at least have an idea of your ancestor's religious denomination, and in most cases you will have to visit a brick and mortar establishment to view them.

Most church records are kept by the individual church, although in some denominations, records are placed in a regional archive or maintained at the diocesan level. Local Historical Societies are sometimes the repository for the state's older church records. Below are links archives that maintain church records, as well as a few databases that can be viewed online.

The **Family History Library** contains many church records from a variety of denominations on microfilm.

Family History Library:
http://familysearch.org/learn/wiki/en/Family_History_Library

Center for Western Studies – Variety of South Dakota Church records from various denominations

P.O. Box 727
Augustana College
Sioux Falls, SD 57197
Phone: (605) 336-4921
Fax: (605) 336-5447

Center for Western Studies: http://www.augie.edu/center-for-western-studies/

Central Repositories for Denominational Records

Church of Jesus Christ of Latter-day Saints (Mormons)

Early Mormon Church records for South Dakota can be found on film located at the LDS Family History Library in Salt Lake City and can be searched via the **Family History Library Catalog**

Family History Library Catalog:
https://familysearch.org/eng/Library/FHLC/frameset_fhlc.asp

Congregational

Congregational Library
14 Beacon Street
Boston, MA 02108
Phone: (617) 523-0470
Fax: (617) 523-0470
E-mail: jsteytler@14beacon.org

Congregational Library: http://www.congregationallibrary.org/

Lutheran

Evangelical Lutheran Church of America (ELCA Archives)
8765 West Higgins Road
Chicago, IL 60631-4198
Phone: (773) 380-2818
E-mail: info@elca.org

Evangelical Lutheran Church of America (ELCA Archives):
http://www.elca.org/archives/

Methodist

Archives and History Library
Dakotas Conference
United Methodist Church
1331 West University Boulevard
Mitchell, SD 57301
Phone: (605) 996-6552
Fax: (605) 996-1766

Mailing Address:
P.O. Box 460
Mitchell, SD 57301

Dakotas Conference
United Methodist Church: http://www.dakotasumc.org/about-us/history/

Episcopal

The Diocese of South Dakota
500 South Main Avenue
Sioux Falls, South Dakota
57104-6814
Phone: (605) 338-9751
Fax: (605) 336-6243

The Diocese of South Dakota: https://www.diocesesd.org/

Roman Catholic

Diocese of Rapid City
606 Cathedral Drive
Rapid City, SD 57709
Phone: (605) 343-3541

Diocese of Rapid City:http://www.rapidcitydiocese.org/WP/

Diocese of Sioux Falls
523 N. Duluth Ave.
Sioux Falls, SD 57105
Phone: (605) 334-9861

Diocese of Sioux Falls: http://www.diocese-of-sioux-falls.org/

South Dakota Military Records

More than 40 million Americans have participated in some kind of war service since America was colonized. The chance of finding your ancestor amongst those records is exceptionally high. Military records can even reveal individuals who never actually served, such as those who registered for the two World Wars but were never called to duty.

Below are a number of links to websites and archives that contain South Dakota military records.

South Dakota State Archives – Fourth South Dakota Infantry, 1917; 1885 Civil War Veterans Census, Spanish American War roster, WPA Veterans Cemetery Index

900 Governors Drive
Pierre, SD 57501
Phone: (605) 773-3804
Fax: (605) 773-6041
E-mail: archref@state.sd.us

South Dakota State Archives: http://history.sd.gov/Archives/

National Archives at Denver - Revolutionary War records, Pension and bounty land warrant applications

17101 Huron Street
Broomfield, CO 80023
Telephone: 303-604-4740
Fax: 303-407-5707

National Archives at Denver:
http://www.archives.gov/denver/public/genealogy.html

National Archives—Central Plains Region (Kansas City) - selected military service records and indexes; selected pension and bounty-land warrant applications

400 West Pershing Road
Kansas City, MO 64108
Phone: (816) 268-8000

National Archives—Central Plains Region (Kansas City):
http://www.archives.gov/kansas-city/

US Department of Veterans Affairs Nationwide Gravesite Locator – includes information on veterans and their family members buried in veterans and military cemeteries having a government grave marker.

US Department of Veterans Affairs Nationwide Gravesite Locator: http://gravelocator.cem.va.gov/

You may also find your ancestor's military records in the following databases:

United States General Index to Pension Files, 1861-1934:
https://familysearch.org/search/collection/1919699

United States Index to Service Records, War with Spain, 1898:
https://familysearch.org/search/collection/1919583

United States Index to Indian Wars Pension Files, 1892-1926 – military pension records of soldiers who fought in the Indian Wars between 1817 and 1898

United States Index to Indian Wars Pension Files, 1892-1926:
https://familysearch.org/search/collection/1979427

United States Registers of Enlistments in the U.S. Army, 1798-1914 - index of men who enlisted in the United States Army, 1798-1914.

United States Registers of Enlistments in the U.S. Army, 1798-1914: https://familysearch.org/search/collection/1880762

United States Mexican War Pension Index, 1887-1926 - index to Mexican War pension files for service between 1846 and 1848

United States Mexican War Pension Index, 1887-1926: https://familysearch.org/search/collection/1979390

Civil War Soldiers Service Records - Service records for both Union and Confederate soldiers indexed by soldier's name, rank, and unit.

Civil War Soldier Service Records: http://go.fold3.com/civilwar_records/

South Dakota Cemetery Records

As convenient as it is to search cemetery records online, keep in mind that there are a few disadvantages over visiting a cemetery in person. They are:

1. Tombstone information is not always accurately transcribed
2. The arrangement of the graves in a cemetery can be crucial as family members are often buried next to each other or in the same grave. This arrangement is not always preserved in the alphabetical indexes that are found online.

With that information in mind, the following websites have databases that can be searched online for South Dakota Cemetery records.

South Dakota State Archives – Records that were cataloged as part of the WPA Cemetery Project, updated regularly

900 Governors Drive
Pierre, SD 57501
Phone: (605) 773-3804
Fax: (605) 773-6041
E-mail: archref@state.sd.us

South Dakota State Archives:
http://apps.sd.gov/applications/dt58cemetery/

South Dakota Tombstone Transcription Project - death and burial records

South Dakota Tombstone Transcription Project:
http://www.usgwtombstones.org/southdakota/sdakota.html

African American Cemeteries Online – African American, slave, and Native American cemetery records

African American Cemeteries Online:
http://africanamericancemeteries.com/

Access Genealogy – database of South Dakota cemetery record transcriptions

Access Genealogy:
http://www.accessgenealogy.com/cemetery/south-dakota-cemetery-records.htm

Find a Grave – over 100 million grave records can be searched on this site. Search can be conducted by name, location, or cemetery name.

Find a Grave: http://www.findagrave.com/

Interment.net - A free online database containing approximately 4 million cemetery records from around the world.

Interment.net link to: http://www.interment.net/

Billion Graves – as the name implies, you can search a billion records including headstone photos, transcriptions, cemetery records, and grave locations.

Billion Graves:
http://billiongraves.com/pages/search/index.php#cemetery

South Dakota Obituaries

Obituaries can reveal a wealth about our ancestor and other relatives. You can search our **South Dakota Obituaries Listings** from hundreds of South Dakota newspapers online for free.

South Dakota Obituaries Listings:
http://obituarieshelp.org/south_dakota_newspaper_obituaries.html

South Dakota Wills and Probate Records

The documents found in a probate packet may include a complete inventory of a person's estate, newspaper entries, witness testimony, a copy of a will, list of debtors and creditors, names of executors or trustees, names of heirs. They can not only tell you about the ancestor you're currently researching, but lead to other ancestors.

South Dakota State Archives – Territorial Era probate records

900 Governors Drive
Pierre, SD 57501
Phone: (605) 773-3804
Fax: (605) 773-6041
E-mail: archref@state.sd.us

South Dakota State Archives: http://history.sd.gov/Archives/

Probate records created since statehood in 1889 can be found at
South Dakota Clerk of Court Offices

South Dakota Clerk of Court Offices:
http://ujs.sd.gov/Contact/clerkcourts.aspx

Family Search has the following indexes that can be searched online for free:

South Dakota, Minnehaha County, Probate Case Records, 1873-1935: https://familysearch.org/search/collection/1392773

South Dakota Immigration and Naturalization Records

The naturalization process generated many types of records, including petitions, declarations of intention, and oaths of allegiance. These records can provide family historians with information such as a person's birth date and place of birth, immigration year, marital status, spouse information, occupation, witnesses' names and addresses, and more.

South Dakota State Archives – All naturalization records for South Dakota

900 Governors Drive
Pierre, SD 57501
Phone: (605) 773-3804
Fax: (605) 773-6041
E-mail: archref@state.sd.us

South Dakota State Archives: **http://history.sd.gov/Archives/**

National Archives—Central Plains Region (Kansas City) – Federal naturalization records fro South Dakota, North Dakota and Dakota Territory

400 West Pershing Road
Kansas City, MO 64108
Phone: (816) 268-8000

National Archives—Central Plains Region (Kansas City): http://www.archives.gov/kansas-city/finding-aids/naturalization-records.html

Family Search has the following index which can be searched online for free:

South Dakota, County Naturalization Records, 1865-1972: https://familysearch.org/search/collection/2078640

South Dakota Native American Records

South Dakota State Archives – Large collection of Native American resources

900 Governors Drive
Pierre, SD 57501
Phone: (605) 773-3804
Fax: (605) 773-6041
E-mail: archref@state.sd.us

South Dakota State Archives: http://history.sd.gov/Archives/

National Archives at Denver - Indian censuses

17101 Huron Street
Broomfield, CO 80023
Telephone: 303-604-4740
Fax: 303-407-5707

National Archives at Denver:
http://www.archives.gov/denver/public/genealogy.html

National Archives—Central Plains Region (Kansas City) -
Censuses and land allotment files for Native Americans.

400 West Pershing Road
Kansas City, MO 64108
Phone: (816) 268-8000

National Archives—Central Plains Region (Kansas City):
http://www.archives.gov/kansas-city/

Access Genealogy – South Dakota Native American census records, tribal histories, and much more

Access Genealogy: http://www.accessgenealogy.com/native/south-dakota-indian-tribes.htm

U.S. National Archives - information on American Indians who maintained their ties to Federally-recognized Tribes (1830-1970).

U.S. National Archives: http://www.archives.gov/research/native-americans/

Records of the Bureau of Indian Affairs (BIA)

Records of the Bureau of Indian Affairs (BIA): http://www.archives.gov/research/guide-fed-records/groups/075.html

American Indians Records Repository - records dating from the 1700s including trust, education and other historic Indian Affairs records

American Indian Records Repository
Meritex Enterprises
17501 West 98th Street
Lenexa, KS 66219
Phone: 913-888-0601

American Indians Records Repository: http://www.doi.gov/ost/records_mgmt/american-indian-records-repository.cfm

Missing Matriarchs – Resources for Researching Female South Dakota Ancestors

Looking for female ancestors requires an adjustment of how we view traditional records sources. A woman's identity was often under that of her husband, and often individual records for them can be difficult to locate. The following resources are effective in locating female ancestors in South Dakota where traditional records may not reveal them.

Bibliographies

1. *The Divorce Mill: Realistic Sketches of the South Dakota Divorce Colony,* Harry, Hazel, and S.L. Lewis (Sheed and Ward, 1987)
2. *After the West Was Won: Homesteaders and Town-Builders in Western South Dakota, 1900-1917,* Paula M. Nelson (University of Iowa Press, 1978)
3. *Black Hill Ladies: The Frail and the Fair,* Irma Klock (The Author, 1980)
4. *What This Awl Means: Feminist Archaeology at the Wahpeton Dakota Village,* Janet D. Spector (Minnesota Historical Society, 1993)
5. *Daughters of Dakota,* 6 Vols., Sally R. Wagner (Sky Carrier, 1990)

Selected Resources for South Dakota Women's History

Center for Western Studies
Mikkelsen Library
Augustana College
29th and Summit Ave.
Sioux Falls, SD 57197

Women's Studies Program
South Dakota State University
Political Science Department
Brookings, SD 57007

I.D. Weeks Library
Richardson Archives
University of South Dakota
Spearfish, SD 57069

Common South Dakota Surnames

The following surnames are among the most common in South Dakota and are also being currently researched by other genealogists. If you find your surname here, there is a chance that some research has already been performed on your ancestor.

Abbott, Adams, Addy, Ahrenlt, Alden, Algoe, Alice, Allen, Allie, Amelia, Anderson, Ann, Anna, Anne, Anstye, Appleton, Archer, Armentrout, Armstrong, Arnold, Arthur, Artingstall, Atwood, Aufricht, Bailey, Bailey-Wood, Baker, Baldwin, Baliow, Ball, Ballantyne, Ballew, Banwell, Barber, Barnes, Bayly, Beatrice, Bernard, Beverly, Bigge, Bird, Bishop, Black, Blackmore, Blanche, Bonneau, Bonsoll, Bowen, Briggs, Brokaw, Brown, Bullock, Bunch, Burman, Burnham, Busan, Bush, Cal, Cameron, Carol, Caroline, Carr, Celia, Chapman, Charity, Charlotte, Chase, Chris, Christenson, Christie, Church, Clara, Clark, Cody, Coleman, Collins, Comer, Conner, Cooke, Cooper, Cowen, Crawford, Crees, Crispe, Cross, Curswell, Custard, Dare, Davies, Day, Debbie, Derickson, Derrickson, Dibble, Dorward, Dowling, Dulin, Dunn, Dutton, Dyana, Easterick, Edmiston, Edwards, Elder, Elizabeth, Elliott, Ethel, Evans, Evensen, Evonne, Fackleman, Faircluff, Fairholm, Fairservice, Fishel, Fisk, Fiske, Flannery, Fletcher, Francis, French, Frey, Fry, Gardner, Garnet, Garrison, Gilbert, Gladback, Golden, Goodhue, Goodings, Gould, Granby, Graves, Grawell, Greenfield, Griffen, Griggs, Guthrie, Gwinnell, Habben, Hall, Ham, Haney, Hannah, Harbough, Harryman, Hegglund, Helen, Helgeson, Henderson, Hendricks, Hewitt, Hiams, Hicks, Hilary, Hill, Hoag, Holbrook, Hole, Holland, Hood, Hooper, Hopkins, Hoseth, Hoskins, Hubbard, Huber, Humphreys, Huron, Huston, Irion, Isnogle, Iverton, Jarvis, Jeffery, Jeffs, Jenkins, Jennie, Jennifer, Jergens, Jerome, Joan, Johnson, Jones, Jordan, Joyce, Judd, Julius, Kantor, Kate, Katherine, Kerr, Kiefer, Kielhorn, Kim, Kimball, Kimpson, King, Kirkpatric, Kjolseth, Knight, Kurtz, Laura, Leavitt, Leonard, Lina, Livingston, Long, Loobey, Lush, Lynne, Mabel, Magdaline, Manchester, Margaret, Margery, Marie, Martin, Mary, Masterson, Matthews, Mattie, Maxie, Maybury, McBane, McClain, McKee, McMerrick, McNeil, McNutt, Means, Mehitable, Messerly, Metcalf, Middlesworth, Miles, Millard, Miller, Mills, Morgan, Mork, Morley, Morrow, Mullimaxone, Myers,

Nancy, Nedrow, Neeley, Nelson, Newberry, Nichols, Nighswonger, Noorda, Norman, Notestine, Nussbaum, Oswalt, Paine, Palmer, Panko, Parks, Parsons, Payter, Pearson, Peck, Peggy, Perlina, Peterson, Phylis, Pierce, Pierpont, Pike, Pinchard, Pool, Porter, Potter, Pottorff, Poulson, Powers, Pratt, Pugh, Pulman, Rambo, Rane, Reardon, Rebecca, Reed, Regan, Reinhold, Remember, Resner, Rheborg, Rice, Richards, Rinehart, Ripley, Robbins, Roberts, Rodgers, Rogers, Roher, Rohrer, Rominger, Rose, Roush, Ryburn, Saha, Sammons, Sampson, Sarah, Sawvel, Schaich, Schiefelben, Schmalle, Schumacher, Schuyler, Scott, Service, Shaaron, Sharp, Shaul, Sheldon, Shell, Sheryl, Siedschlaw, Siemsen, Simmons, Smith, Smyth, Snow, Son, Spiller, Stanberry, Stanley, Steenson, Stephenson, Still, Stoddart, Stoecer, Stone, Stowe, Strong, Susan, Swanlund, Swift, Symonds, Talley, Taylor, Thatcher, Thompson, Thurston, Thyer, Tolley, Trowbridge, Trumbell, Tumock, Tuttle, Upshaw, Van Dreser, Verna, Vik, Vogel, Wakefield, Wallace, Walters, Waltz, Ward, Warner, Webster, Weiersheuser, Welton, Wheeldon, Whipple, Whistler, Whitcomb, White, Whitman, Wilder, Wilkinson, Williams, Wilson, Zenishek, Ziegler, Zook

About the Author

Gary L. Morris worked from 2009 to 2014 as a professional researcher for a major player in the genealogy field. After tracing his family lineage back to 1683, he found that genealogy could be an expensive undertaking. As such, has decided to publish these helpful guides to share the valuable free information he has discovered during his career to help others trace their family lineages as inexpensively as possible. An avid genealogist himself, he hopes you will find this guide factual, thorough, helpful, and most of all, effective in helping you to find your family members.

Notes

Notes

www.ingramcontent.com/pod-product-compliance
Lightning Source LLC
Chambersburg PA
CBHW061927280526
45787CB00004B/1513